Over The Horizon

Yvette Thomas-Trotter

PUBLISHED BY DiViNE PURPOSE PUBLISHING
WWW.DIVINEPURPOSEPUBLISHING.COM
INFO@DIVINEPURPOSEPUBLISHING.COM
(866) 211-7637 Ext. 0

ISBN-13:978-0692525227
ISBN-10: 069252522X

PRINTED IN THE UNITED STATES OF AMERICA

Thank You

To God be the glory for never allowing me to give up on my dreams, and for all His love.

To my husband Carl Trotter and my 3 children; Crystal, Eugene and Marcus

To my brother Wilbon Robinson for pushing and encouraging me.

To Evelyn Espinosa, Thank you for being there for me, for encouraging me and teaching me the Word of God, I love you

To Divine Purpose Publishing Company for the wonderful work they have done.

This Special Gift You Cannot Buy

THIS SPECIAL GIFT YOU CANNOT BUY,
FOR IT WAS PAID IN FULL WHEN MY MASTER DIED.

NO MONEY, NO CAR, NO HOUSE, NO TREASURER
CAN EVER COME UP TO THE COST,
THIS GIFT MEASURE.

YOU NEED NOT A DOLLAR, A DIME OR A CENT,
JUST TURN FROM YOUR SINS AND TRULY REPENT.

FOR THIS GIFT IS SOMETHING YOU CANNOT BUY,
FOR IT WAS PAID IN FULL WHEN MY MASTER DIED.

God's Servant

YOU WORK SO HARD FOR YOUR MASTER ABOVE,
PREACHING THE GOSPEL WITH KINDNESS AND LOVE.

YOU'RE PATIENCE AND YOU'RE CARING—
THEY PLAY A GREAT PART,
WITH LOVE AND MERCY
THAT COMES FROM YOUR HEART.

WE SOMETIMES HAVE PROBLEMS WE DON'T
UNDERSTAND
BUT PASTOR YOU ARE ALWAYS WILLING TO LEND A
HELPING HAND. WHEN YOU TEACH US GOD'S
WORD YOU LET THE HOLY GHOST GUIDE, NOT A
WORD SUGAR COATED, NOT A WORD DO YOU HIDE.

YOU TEACH GOD'S PEOPLE
NOT LEADING ONE ASTRAY,

You give us His Word
in order to keep His way.

We appreciate you Pastor
and we want you to know
We thank God for you
and we truly love you so.

Praise Him

WE KNOW HOW GOD HAS KEPT US
THROUGH THE MONTH, YEARS AND DAYS,
YET WE REFUSED TO GIVE
OUR FATHER LORD HIS GLORIOUS PRAISE.

HE KEEPS US FROM ALL EVIL,
AND ANSWERS WHEN WE CALL.
HE PLACED US ON A SOLID ROCK,
AND CATCHES US BEFORE WE FALL.

HE FILLS US WITH HIS SPIRIT,
AND GUIDES US ALONG THE WAY,
HE WOKE US UP THIS MORNING
TO SEE A BRAND NEW DAY.

SO LET EVERYTHING THAT HAS BREATH PRAISE OUR
FATHER GOD ABOVE, FOR ALL THE PRAISE IS DUE
UNTO HIM OUR MASTER AND SAVIOR—
GOD OF LOVE.

A Special Friend

I asked the Lord above
To send me a friend so dear.

Someone I could talk to,
And someone that truly cares.

When He looked down from above,
He looked upon me and you.

And bound us together,
what a special friendship so true.

For our friendship I treasure
Deep down within my heart,
Hoping we'll be friends forever
And never stray apart.

I Must Witness

I must witness to others wherever I go.
I must witness to others,
So others may know.

Jesus our Savior has died for the lost.
For He paid the price on Calvary Cross.

I must witness to others
in order to share God's Love.

I must witness to others,
for that Commandment came
from our God and Savior above.

Life Rose Early One Morning

They hung Him on the cross one day,
for something He didn't do,
They said he claims He's the son of God
and also King of the Jews.

They whipped Him, spit on Him
And also pulled His beard.

They treated Him like a sinner man
And no one ever cared.

One soldier pierced Him in His side
To see if He was dead
But He had already gave up the ghost,
And so He hung His head.

They took His body to the tomb,
In order to rest Him there.

SOME WERE HAPPY, SOME WERE SAD
AND SOME REALLY DIDN'T CARE.

HE ROSE THE THIRD DAY— MORNING
JUST LIKE HE SAID HE WOULD
AND WHEN HE ROSE THAT MORNING
HE ROSE FOR ME AND YOU.

Your Soul

Your soul
is the most precious gift you have
within your being.

More precious
than any wealth
or anything you've ever seen.

It's precious and it's eternal
For your soul never dies

One day we all must stand before our God,
one day we all must rise.

The Wonders of God

LOOK AT THE WONDERFUL THINGS GOD HAS DONE
HE CREATED THE MOON AND STARS AND THE SUN.

LOOK AT THE PLANETS HE PLACED SO HIGH
FAR UP YONDER IN THE BIG BLUE SKY.

LOOK AT THE FISHES IN THE DEEP BLUE SEA
THE FLOWERS THE ANIMALS AND THE BIG TALL
TREES.

LOOK AT THE WONDERS THAT GOD HAS DONE.
JUST LOOK…
JUST LOOK…
JUST LOOK ALL AROUND.

The Deliverer

Is your body in sickness,
you're at the end of your rope?

The doctor gave you up,
and said there is no hope?

Is your rent behind and your light bill due?

Your phone cut off and your car is too?

Are there problems at home
or in your spiritual life?

Problems with your husband,
children or wife?

Well,
the deliverer is here to set you free,
For He said cast all your cares,
cast them all on Me.

The Greatest of These is Charity

LOVE SAVED MY WRETCHED SOUL ONE DAY.
AND GUIDE MY FOOTSTEPS ALONG THE WAY.

LOVE HAS THE POWER IN HIS HAND,
TO SAVE THE SINFUL WRETCHED MAN.

LOVE LOOKED DOWN AND SAW MY SINS,
STRETCH FORTH HIS HANDS AND TOOK ME IN.

LOVE LET ME KNOW MY SINS ARE FORGIVEN
AND NOW I HAVE A REASON FOR LIVING.

WHENEVER I NEED HIM, HE'S ALWAYS THERE.

FOR LOVE IS SOMEONE I KNOW THAT TRULY CARES
WHATEVER THE PROBLEM HE WILL UNDERSTAND,
FOR LOVE IS ALWAYS WILLING TO LEND A HAND.

SOMETIMES LOVE SEEMS SO FAR AWAY,
BUT I KNOW I CAN REACH HIM IF I ONLY PRAY.

FOR LOVE IS MY DEAR AND MERCIFUL FRIEND

WHO SAID

"LO I WILL BE WITH YOU EVEN UNTO THE END."

SO IF YOU NEED LOVE AND I KNOW YOU DO.
TRY JESUS AND YOU'LL SEE HE'S THE ONE FOR YOU.

A Quiet Moment

AS I SAT IN THE PARK BY THE WATER SIDE,
I CAN SEE THE BEAUTIFUL OCEAN
THAT IS ALSO WIDE.

AS I LISTENED TO THE WAVES I COULD HEAR
THE BIRDS CHIRPING
AS THEY FLEW THROUGH THE AIR.

THE COOL WIND BLEW
AND WITH THE COOL BREEZE
I SHIVER AND SHAKE.

BUT EVEN WITH THE COOL BREEZE,
A QUIET MOMENT WE ALL MUST TAKE.

A Virtuous Woman

VIRTUOUS WOMAN
IS A GIFT THAT WAS GIVEN TO MEN,

TO LOVE HONOR AND CHERISH
AND TO WALK HAND IN HAND.

SHE WAS GIVEN TO MEN TO WALK BY HIS SIDE,

FOR WHOM THE LORD HAS JOIN TOGETHER
NO MAN CAN DIVIDE.

Heart to Heart

YOU WAITED SO LONG FOR THIS MOMENT TO PASS,
THIS MOMENT THAT SEEMS FOREVER THIS MOMENT
THAT SEEMS WOULD LAST FOREVER.

FOR THE TIME HAS COME TO FACE THIS LIFE,
NO LONGER TWO HEARTS BUT AS MAN AND WIFE.

THOUGH PROBLEMS AND HEARTACHES YOU MAY
SOMETIMES HAVE, YOU MUST HANG IN THERE AND
NEVER GIVE UP. THROUGH THE GOOD AND THE BAD.

FOR YOU PROMISE TO STAY TOGETHER
IN SICKNESS AND IN HEALTH,
FOR BETTER OR FOR WORSE,
IN POVERTY OR IN WEALTH.

FOR YOU'RE BOUND TOGETHER
NO LONGER APART,
THE DECISION WAS YOURS
TO BE BOUND HEART TO HEART.

AND SOMEDAY WHEN THE RAIN REFUSE TO STOP.
AND THE SUN REFUSES TO SHINE.
LOOK TO JESUS YOUR SAVIOR,
AND COMFORT YOU WILL FIND.

True Love

MY HEART THAT ONCE SEEMED
SO EMPTY AND COLD,

IS NOW FULL OF LOVE
DEEP DOWN WITHIN MY SOUL.

FOR TRUE LOVE WITHIN ME I CAN FEEL,
BECAUSE IT CAME FROM
MY SAVIOR GOD
SO I KNOW THIS LOVE IS REAL.

Searching for Peace

COULD SOMEONE PLEASE TELL ME
WHERE I CAN FIND PEACE?
FOR I WILL SEARCH,
AND SEARCH AND I WON'T EVER CEASE.

MR. DOPE COULD YOU PLEASE TELL ME
WHERE HE COULD BE FOUND?

FOR I'VE SEARCHED ALL OVER
AND HE'S NO WHERE AROUND.

"I HAVE THAT PEACE DEAR CHILD
SO YOU DON'T HAVE TO WORRY.
COME GET THIS PEACE
MY CHILD COME GET IT IN A HURRY."

BUT I'VE TRIED YOU BEFORE AND THERE WAS NO
PEACE, SO I WILL CONTINUE TO SEARCH
AND I WON'T EVER CEASE.

FOR WHEN I TRIED YOU,
IT WAS MISERY AND SIN.
NOTHING BUT HEARTACHES
AND MORE PROBLEMS WITHIN.

YOU OFTEN MADE ME PARANOID
WITH DEPRESSION FOLLOWED BEHIND,
YET THERE WAS NO SATISFACTION,
AND NO PEACE I COULD FIND.

LORD,
COULD YOU PLEASE TELL ME
WHERE I COULD FIND PEACE?

FOR I'LL SEARCH AND I'LL SEARCH
AND I WON'T NEVER CEASE.

MY DEAR CHILD
I KNOW WHERE PEACE COULD BE FOUND,
JUST SURRENDER TO ME AND HAVE PEACE ALL
AROUND.

FOR THE PEACE I WILL GIVE TO YOU,
NO MAN CAN TAKE AWAY.
SURRENDER TO ME AND HAVE PEACE TODAY.

Street Walker

AS HE WALKED THE STREETS
WITH A FLOWER IN HIS HAND.
HE DROPPED THE PETALS AS HE WALKED ALONG.

NO DECENT CLOTHES ON HIS BACK
OR NO SHOES ON HIS FEET.
NO MONEY IN HIS POCKET AND NO FOOD TO EAT.
HE WANDERS THROUGH THE CITY TO AND FRO,
NOT A BED TO SLEEP IN, OR A WARM PLACE TO GO.

HE SEARCHES FOR A PLACE TO SLEEP
AS IT DREW NEAR DARK.

ON THE BUS BENCH,
THE SIDEWALK, OR EVEN IN THE PARK.
AS THE COLD WIND BLEW BETWEEN THE BOXES HE
HOVER, WITH A ROCK FOR HIS PILLOW
AND NEWSPAPER FOR HIS COVER.

Keep Me O'Lord

KEEP ME O'LORD
DEAR GOD I PRAY,

PROTECT ME A LONG LIFE'S NARROW WAY.

KEEP ME SAFE FROM HURT AND HARM,
GUIDE ME WITH YOUR LOVING ARMS.

WHEN I'M FALLING PLEASE LEND A HAND,
LEAD AND GUIDE ME AND HELP ME TO STAND.

SO KEEP ME O'LORD DEAR GOD I PRAY,
PLEASE PROTECT ME ALONG LIFE'S NARROW WAY.

Did You Know...
That You Are Loved?

DID YOU KNOW THAT YOU ARE LOVED?
AND THAT THIS SPECIAL LOVE CAME FROM ABOVE.

DID YOU KNOW HE SEES YOUR TEARS?
AND KNOWS THE BURDEN AND HURTS YOU BEAR.

DID YOU KNOW HE SEES YOU LATE AT NIGHT?
CRYING IN THE DARK
BECAUSE NOTHING SEEMS RIGHT.

SO IF YOU DIDN'T KNOW BEFORE,
NOW YOU KNOW YOU ARE LOVED,
AND THIS SPECIAL LOVE, COMES FROM
YOUR FATHER AND SAVIOR GOD ABOVE

Thank You Dear Father

THANK YOU DEAR FATHER
FOR WHAT YOU HAVE DONE.

THANK YOU DEAR FATHER
FOR YOUR ONE AND ONLY SON.

THANK YOU DEAR FATHER
FOR SENDING HIM TO EARTH.

THANK YOU DEAR FATHER
FOR MY DEAR SAVIORS BIRTH.

THANK YOU DEAR FATHER
FOR ON THE CROSS HE DIED.

THANK YOU DEAR FATHER
FOR HIM ABIDING BY MY SIDE.

THANK YOU DEAR FATHER
FOR THE LOVE YOU HAVE GIVEN

Thank you dear father
because of my Savior's love
life is worth living.

Don't Look Back

THOUGH MY MOUNTAIN SEEMS HIGH
AND MY VALLEY SOMETIMES LOW,
I MUST NOT LOOK BACK FOR FORWARD I MUST GO.

FOR THERE'S A CROWN UP AHEAD
WAITING THERE JUST FOR ME.

FOR MY FATHER AND MY LORD
MY EYES WILL SOMEDAY SEE.

FOR THOSE PEARLY GATES
WILL ONE DAY OPEN WIDE
AND I WILL REST MY WEARY HEAD
BY MY MASTER AND SAVIOR'S SIDE.

SO, THOUGH MY MOUNTAIN SEEMS HIGH
AND MY VALLEY SOMETIMES LOW,
I MUST NOT LOOK BACK FOR FORWARD I MUST GO.

Truth

TRUTH IS SOMETHING
THAT SHOULD ALWAYS BE TOLD.
TRUTH IS MORE PRECIOUS THAN SILVER AND GOLD.
TRUTH AND HONESTY WILL NEVER FAIL,
FOR TRUTH SHOULD BE TOLD INSTEAD OF TALE.

Lord, Hear My Prayer

FATHER, LORD, PLEASE HEAR MY PRAYER,
AND LET IT REACH THY LOVING EAR.
I ASK DEAR LORD PLEASE HEAR AND DO,
FOR ALL I WANT IS TO BE MORE LIKE YOU.

Our Merciful Savior Jesus

WHEN THE CARES OF THIS WORLD
SEEM TOO HARD TO BEAR,
TURN IT OVER TO OUR MERCIFUL SAVIOR JESUS

WHEN THE STORMS OF THIS WORLD
RISE UP AND NO ONE SEEMS TO CARE,
TURN IT OVER TO OUR MERCIFUL SAVIOR JESUS

WHEN YOUR BURDENS ARE HEAVY
AND YOUR HEART SOMETIMES ACHE,
TURN IT OVER TO OUR MERCIFUL SAVIOR JESUS

WHEN YOUR SUNSHINE IS DARKENING
AND YOUR BLUE SKIES TURN TO RAIN,
TURN IT OVER TO OUR MERCIFUL SAVIOR JESUS

WHOSE MERCY LAST FROM
EVERLASTING TO EVERLASTING?

NO ONE BUT OUR MERCIFUL SAVIOR JESUS.

True Happiness Within

TRUE HAPPINESS WITHIN
NO SINNER CAN FIND
NO TRUE LOVE, NO JOY,
NO SOUND PEACE OF MIND.

SORROW AND HEARTACHE, MISERY WITHIN
NOTHING BUT SADNESS, HURT AND SIN.
BUT THERE IS SOMEONE KNOCKING,
PLEASE LET ME IN

SURRENDER TO ME
AND HAVE HAPPINESS WITHIN.

Not Just Christmas

CHRISTMAS IS A SPECIAL TIME,
A WONDERFUL TIME OF YEAR.

A TIME FOR LOVE
A TIME FOR GIVING
AND ALSO A TIME TO SHARE.

CHRISTMAS IS A SPECIAL TIME
TO BE WITH THE ONES YOU LOVE,
TO FOLD YOUR HANDS,
AND BEND YOUR KNEES
AND THANK YOUR GOD ABOVE.

BUT CHRISTMAS IS NOT JUST A TIME TO SHOW
OTHERS THAT YOU CARE, FOR LOVE IS SOMETHING
THAT SHOULD BE SHOWN, NOT ONLY AT CHRISTMAS
BUT ALL THROUGH THE YEAR.

God's Mercy

THE MERCY OF GOD
WE DON'T UNDERSTAND,
NO ONE UNDERSTANDS HIS MERCIFUL HAND.

HIS MERCY IS EVERLASTING
FOR THERE IS NO END,
NO ONE CAN UNDERSTAND,
NO ONE CAN TRULY COMPREHEND.

While I Sleep

OH LORD
AS I LAY MY WEARY BODY DOWN TO SLEEP,
PROTECT ME DEAR FATHER
AND MY LIFE MASTER I ASK YOU TO KEEP.

GIVE ME REST LORD THROUGH THE NIGHT,
THAT I MAY RISE AND SEE A NEW MORNING LIGHT.

Searching for a Home

MY FATHER AND MY SAVIOR IS SEARCHING FOR
A HOME. A HOME IN WHICH THEY CAN DWELL IN,
A HOME IN WHICH THEY CAN FREELY ROAM.

IT NEED NOT TO BE FANCY, PAINTED,
VARNISHED OR NEW.
JUST A SIMPLE PLACE TO DWELL IN,
ANY LITTLE PLACE WOULD DO.

NO NEED FOR A SWIMMING POOL,
PATIO, OR FLOWERY YARD.
NO DEN, NO FIREPLACE OR
EVEN THE WINDOW BARRED.

IT NEED NOT TO BE A HOME
THAT SITS ON FIFTH OR PARK AVENUE

JUST A SIMPLE HOME TO DWELL IN,
A LITTLE HOME WILL DO

IT NEED NOT A BUTLER,
A MAID OR A HOST.

JUST THE HELP OF HIS ONLY SON
AND THE POWER OF THE HOLY GHOST.

SO IF YOU'RE READY TO SURRENDER
AND TURN FROM YOUR SINS
MY FATHER HIS SON AND THE HOLY GHOST
ARE NOW READY TO MOVE IN.

Sit Still

SIT STILL AND HEAR HIS VOICE OF LOVE,
FOR NO ONE HAS A VOICE LIKE OUR MASTER ABOVE.

SIT STILL AND LISTEN
FOR HIS VOICE YOU WILL HEAR,
THE VOICE OF A SAVIOR THAT TRULY CARES.

SIT STILL AND LISTEN
FOR ENCOURAGING WORDS OF PEACE,
FOR HIS MERCY AND LOVE SHALL NEVER CEASE.

SIT STILL...
SIT STILL...
JUST SIT STILL...

Please Open Your Heart …
and Let Me In

PLEASE OPEN YOUR HEART AND LET ME IN,
SURRENDER TO ME AND TURN FROM YOUR SINS

I DIED FOR YOUR SOUL
SO YOU WOULDN'T BE LOST
FOR I PAID FOR YOUR SINS ON CALVARY CROSS

MY CHILD MY PRECIOUS CHILD
I CAN'T FORCE MYSELF IN
FOR IF I COULD I WOULD ENTER
AND WASH AWAY YOUR SINS.

IT HURTS ME SO MUCH TO SEE YOU THIS WAY.
BUT THE DECISION IS YOURS
YOU MUST MAKE IT TODAY.
FOR TOMORROW MY CHILD MAY BE TOO LATE.
FOR YOUR LIFE MAY COME TO A CLOSE
AND SO WILL HEAVENS GATE.

Rain Drop

THE RAINDROPS FALLING SOFTLY TO THE GROUND.
AS A TRICKLE DOWN THE WINDOW PANE
AND ALL AROUND.

THE FLOWERS AND THE TREES
ARE ONCE MORE REVISED
FOR THE RAIN DROPS FROM OUR FATHER
HAS MADE THEM ALIVE.

Birthday Wishes

YOUR BIRTHDAY TIME IS ONCE MORE HERE.
FOR THE LORD HAS BLESSED YOU
TO SEE ANOTHER YEAR.

MAY YOUR WISHES BE GRANTED,
AND YOUR DAY BE GLAD.
HOPING THIS WILL BE
THE BEST BIRTHDAY YOU EVER HAD.

Echo in the Wind

I HEARD A VOICE CRYING
IT ECHOED IN THE WIND.

FROM WHERE IT CAME I KNEW NOT,
I KNOW NOT WHERE IT WAS.

IT SOUNDED LIKE A CHILD CRYING,
A CHILD SO MEEK AND MILD,
A CHILD HUMBLE AND GENTLE,
GOD'S PRECIOUS LITTLE CHILD.

THEY SOUND AS THOUGH
THEY ARE TORMENTED WITH HARSH BITTER PAIN,

BUT MAYBE IT WAS JUST MY IMAGINATION
MAYBE IT WAS ALL IN VAIN.

THE CRY HAS STOPPED NOW,
BUT YET IN MY MIND I WONDER.

WAS THERE SOMETHING
I COULD HAVE DONE TO HELP ?

FOR IN MY MIND
I CAN'T HELP BUT PONDER.

IMAGINATION..MAYBE IT WAS ALL WITHIN,
OR PERHAPS IT WAS JUST A VOICE,
THAT ECHOED IN THE WIND.

Praise and Worship Him

BOW DOWN, WORSHIP, PRAISE AND SING
GIVE GLORY TO OUR SAVIOR, LORD AND KING
THE ALPHA, THE OMEGA,
THE BEGINNING AND THE END
OUR MASTER AND SAVIOR
THE CREATOR OF ALL MEN

SING PRAISES OF THANKSGIVING
AND WORDS FULL OF LOVE

GIVE HONOR AND GLORY TO OUR FATHER ABOVE
PRAISE HIM FOR THE SKY,
MOUNTAINS, VALLEY AND SEAS

PRAISE AND WORSHIP HIM ON ALL BENDING KNEES.
LET EVERYTHING THAT HAS BREATH PRAISE
OUR SAVIOR, LORD AND KING.

RAISE YOUR VOICE, SHOUT FOR JOY.
PRAISE, WORSHIP AND SING.

A Gift From Our Father

A GIFT FROM OUR FATHER
THAT WAS GIVEN TO MEN,
IT WAS WRAPPED
AND DELIVERED BY HIS LOVING HAND

A GIFT FROM HIS HEART THAT WAS FULL OF LOVE,
IT CAME FROM OUR FATHER GOD ABOVE.

A GIFT HE LOVES DEARLY YET WILLING TO SHARE,
A GIFT THAT SHOWS HOW MUCH
OUR FATHER TRULY CARES.

A GIFT THAT WAS PRECIOUS, MEEK AND MILD,
THAT GIFT WAS OUR FATHER'S DEAR SWEET CHILD.

The Gates Are Open

THE GATES ARE OPEN ALL ARE WELCOMED IN
FOR A SAVIOR AND LORD HAS DIED FOR OUR SINS

ALL ARE WELCOMED BY OUR MASTER ABOVE,
ALL ARE WELCOMED WITH OPEN ARMS OF LOVE.

THE GATES ARE OPEN JUST SURRENDER
AND WALK IN
SURRENDER TO JESUS
AND TURN FROM YOUR SINS
THE GATES ARE OPEN
ARE YOU WILLING TO COME AND STAY?

THE GATES ARE OPEN
THE DECISION IS YOURS TODAY.

Who Cares

Who cares what you're going through,
who cares if your health is bad.

Who cares if you're depressed
or even feeling sad.

Who cares if you have no place to live
or no shoes on your feet
or even if you're lonely
and have no food to eat

Who cares?
Who cares about you,
and the things that you do?

Well,
I'll tell you who cares,
who truly cares for you.

the Lord cares, He truly cares for you!

Author Bio

YVETTE (DIANE) THOMAS TROTTER
WAS BORN IN BELIZE CITY CENTRAL AMERICA.
AT THE AGE OF 7 SHE CAME TO THE UNITED STATES

YVETTE GAVE HER LIFE TO THE LORD AT THE AGE
OF 19. EVEN AT A YOUNG AGE SHE ALWAYS ENJOYED
HELPING AND ENCOURAGING OTHERS.

YVETTE NOW RESIDE IN FLORIDA WITH HER
HUSBAND CARL AND 3 KIDS
CRYSTAL, EUGENE AND MARCUS.

Yvette is also a Youth Sunday School
teacher at her church.
There she inspires, encourages and teaches
children the Word of God.

OVER THE HORIZON
BY YVETTE THOMAS-TROTTER

PUBLISHED BY

DIVINE PURPOSE PUBLISHING
EMAIL: INFO@DIVINEPURPOSEPUBLISHING.COM
WEBSITE: WWW.DIVINEPURPOSEPUBLISHING.COM
(866) 211-7637 Ext. 0

Made in United States
Orlando, FL
07 July 2022